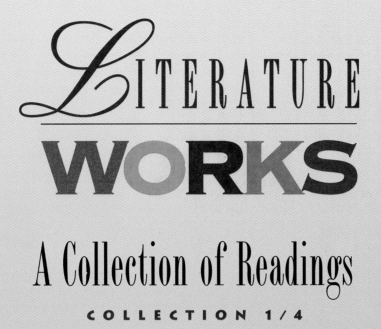

LITERATURE
WORKS

A Collection of Readings

COLLECTION 1/4

Silver Burdett Ginn
A Division of Simon & Schuster
160 Gould Street
Needham Heights, MA 02194

Acknowledgments appear on page 224, which constitutes an extension of this copyright page.

ISBN: 0-663-61219-5   6 7 8 9 10 RRD 03 02 01 00 99 98 97

LITERATURE WORKS

A Collection of Readings

COLLECTION 1 / 4

THEMES

Tell Me A Story

Watch Me Grow!

SILVER BURDETT GINN

Needham, MA   Parsippany, NJ

Atlanta, GA   Deerfield, IL   Irving, TX   Santa Clara, CA

4

Theme

8

Watch Me Grow!

6

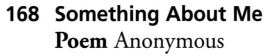

Tell Me A Story

Theme 7 Contents

9

Meet Te Ata and Lynn Moroney

Te Ata is a Chickasaw Indian. She has been a storyteller for many, many years. She is almost 100 years old!

Baby Rattlesnake is her best story.

Lynn Moroney is part Native American. She is also a storyteller. Te Ata let Lynn take her story and make it into a book.

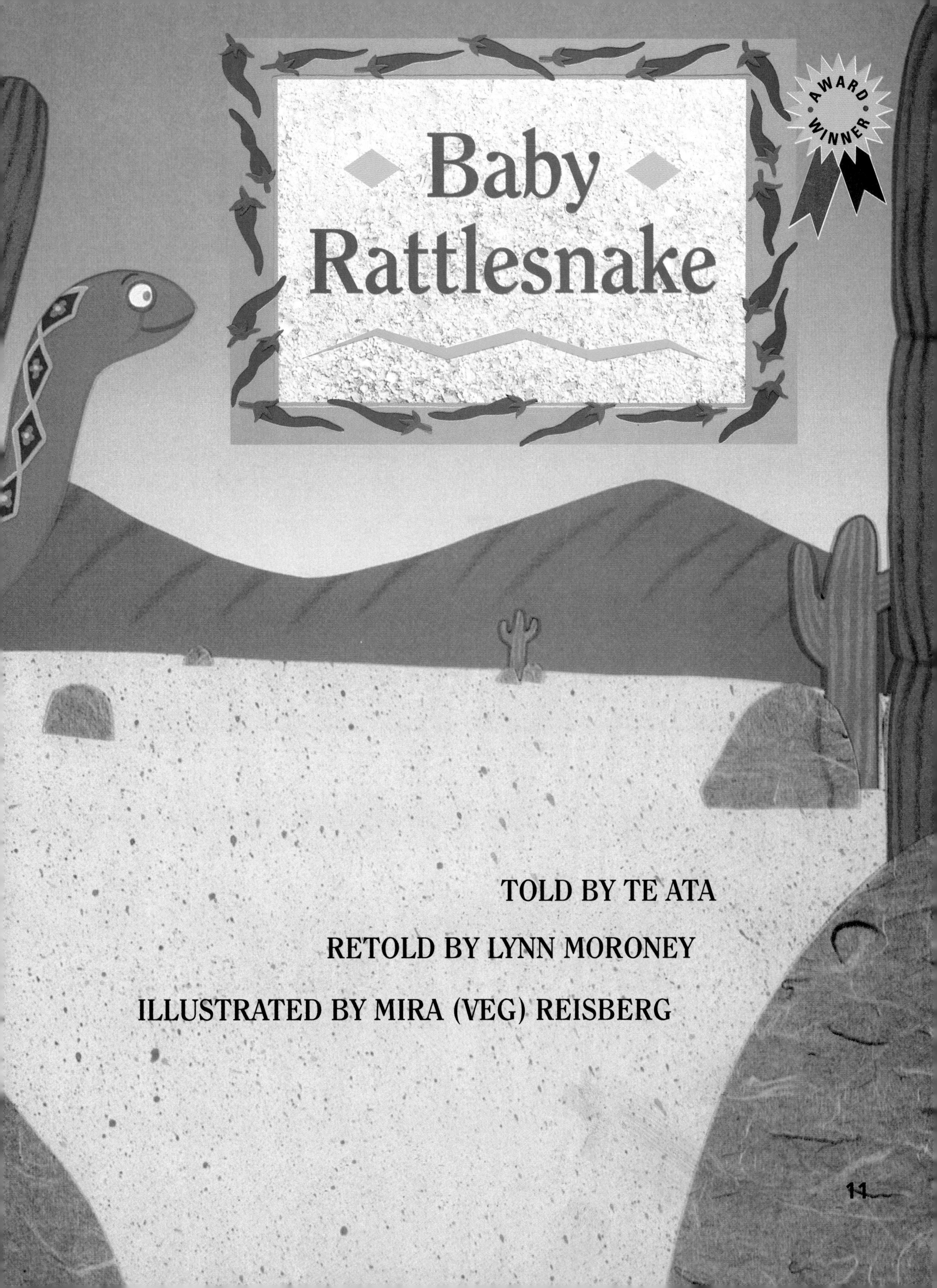

◆ Baby ◆
Rattlesnake

TOLD BY TE ATA

RETOLD BY LYNN MORONEY

ILLUSTRATED BY MIRA (VEG) REISBERG

AWARD WINNER

11

Out in the place where the rattlesnakes lived, there was a little baby rattlesnake who cried all the time because he did not have a rattle.

**H**e said to his mother and father, "I don't know why I don't have a rattle. I'm made just like my brother and sister. How can I be a rattlesnake if I don't have a rattle?"

Mother and Father Rattlesnake said, "You are too young to have a rattle. When you get to be as old as your brother and sister, you will have a rattle, too."

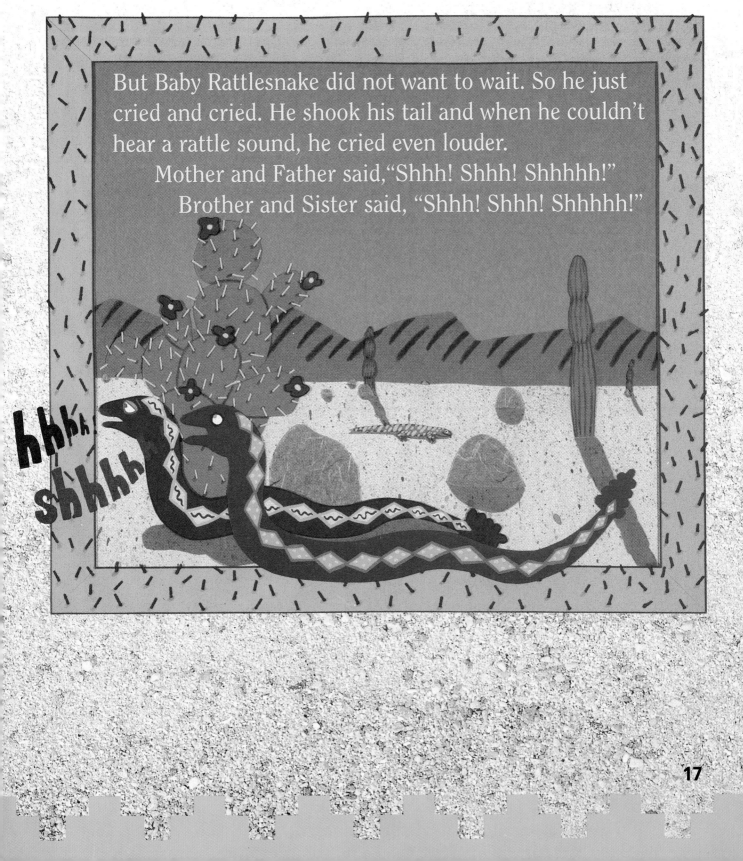

But Baby Rattlesnake did not want to wait. So he just cried and cried. He shook his tail and when he couldn't hear a rattle sound, he cried even louder.

Mother and Father said,"Shhh! Shhh! Shhhhh!"

Brother and Sister said, "Shhh! Shhh! Shhhhh!"

But Baby Rattlesnake wouldn't stop crying. He kept the Rattlesnake People awake all night.

he next morning, the Rattlesnake People called a big council. They talked and they talked just like people do, but they couldn't decide how to make that little baby rattlesnake happy. He didn't want anything else but a rattle.

At last one of the elders said, "Go ahead, give him a rattle. He's too young and he'll get into trouble. But let him learn a lesson. I just want to get some sleep."

So they gave Baby Rattlesnake a rattle.

**B**aby Rattlesnake loved his rattle. He shook his tail and for the first time he heard, "Ch-Ch-Ch! Ch-Ch-Ch!" He was so excited!

He sang a rattle song, "Ch-Ch-Ch! Ch-Ch-Ch!"

He danced a rattle dance, "Ch-Ch-Ch! Ch-Ch-Ch!"

ha ha

Soon Baby Rattlesnake learned to play tricks with his rattle. He hid in the rocks and when the small animals came by, he darted out rattling "Ch-Ch-Ch!" "Ch-Ch-Ch!"

He made Jack Rabbit jump. He made Old Man Turtle jump. He made Prairie Dog jump.

Each time Baby Rattlesnake laughed and laughed. He thought it was fun to scare the animal people.

**M**other and Father warned Baby Rattlesnake, "You must not use your rattle in such a way."

Big Brother and Big Sister said, "You are not being careful with your rattle."

The Rattlesnake People told Baby Rattlesnake to stop acting so foolish with his rattle.

Baby Rattlesnake did not listen.

ne day, Baby Rattlesnake said to his mother and father, "How will I know a chief's daughter when I see her?"

"Well, she's usually very beautiful and walks with her head held high," said Father.

"And she's very neat in her dress," added Mother.

"Why do you want to know?" asked Father.

"Because I want to scare her!" said Baby Rattlesnake. And he started right off down the path before his mother and father could warn him never to do a thing like that.

The little fellow reached the place where the Indians traveled. He curled himself up on a log and he started rattling. "Chh-Chh-Chh!" He was having a wonderful time.

All of a sudden he saw a beautiful maiden coming toward him from a long way off. She walked with her head held high, and she was very neat in her dress.

"Ah," thought Baby Rattlesnake. "She must be the chief's daughter."

**B**aby Rattlesnake hid in the rocks. He was excited. This was going to be his best trick.

He waited and waited. The chief's daughter came closer and closer. When she was in just the right spot, he darted out of the rocks.

"Ch-Ch-Ch-Ch-Ch!"

 o!" cried the chief's daughter. She whirled around, stepping on Baby Rattlesnake's rattle and crushing it to pieces.

Baby Rattlesnake looked at his beautiful rattle scattered all over the trail. He didn't know what to do.

He took off for home as fast as he could.

With great sobs, he told Mother and Father what had happened. They wiped his tears and gave him big rattlesnake hugs.

For the rest of that day, Baby Rattlesnake stayed safe and snug, close by his rattlesnake family.

Baby Rattlesnake wanted a rattle more than anything else. Have you ever wanted something very, very much? What was it?

Draw a picture of something you wanted. Write about why you wanted it.

Te Ata, a Storyteller

Te Ata grew up in Oklahoma. She loved the outdoors. She also enjoyed hearing stories and reading books.

Te Ata's love of nature and stories came from her parents. Her mother told her the names of all of the plants that grew in the forest.

In the evenings, her father would tell Chickasaw stories to his nine children.

Te Ata telling a tale in Santa Fe

When Te Ata grew up, she told many Native American stories. She loved teaching others about the life of her people.

Te Ata's name means "One Who Brings the Morning." She has brought much sunshine to people by telling her stories.

CLAY STORYTELLERS

These pictures show storyteller dolls made of clay. There are many different kinds.

A man playing an instrument

contemporary, Helen Cordero
Cochiti Pueblo, U.S.A.

A mother singing to a child

contemporary, Helen Cordero
Cochiti Pueblo, U.S.A.

A woman with children

contemporary, Rose Pecos
Jemez Pueblo, U.S.A.

A grandfather telling
a story

contemporary, Helen Cordero
Cochiti Pueblo, U.S.A.

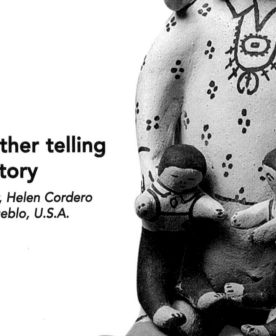

Meet the Authors and Illustrator

Marjorie and **Mitchell Sharmat** often work together when writing children's stories. Marjorie started writing when she was eight. Mitchell began writing when he was seven. They're not the only writers in their family. Their sons have written books for children, too.

Esther Baran read and drew pictures all the time as a child. Her mother had to pry the books from her hands to get her to go outside to play. She draws pictures for folk tales. Russian folk tales were the first ones she chose to do.

Stone Soup

a play by

Marjorie and Mitchell Sharmat

CHARACTERS

First Traveler

First Woman

First Man

Second Traveler

Second Woman

Second Man

Third Traveler

Third Woman

Third Man

Narrator

Other People of the Village

Setting: The story takes place in a Russian village many years ago.

48

Narrator: Three travelers were on their way home. They walked through woods. They walked through meadows. They walked for many miles.

First Traveler: I need to eat.

Second Traveler: I need to sleep.

Third Traveler: I need to eat and sleep.

Narrator: Late in the day the travelers came to a village. The people in that village saw the three travelers coming down the road. The people thought how tired and hungry the travelers looked. But they had very little food for themselves.

First Man: Those travelers will want food to eat and a place to sleep. What can we do?

Second Man: Tell them the wolf ate all our food! Then we can hide it.

First Woman: Good idea! We can hide it in lots of different places.

Narrator: The people ran to hide their food. Soon the three travelers entered the town.

First Traveler: We have walked and walked. May we have some food and a place to sleep?

Third Man: A wolf ate all our food. All we have is water.

Second Traveler: Water! Good! We can make stone soup with that.

First Woman: What is stone soup?

First Traveler: We will show you. Find us a big pot. Then bring us some water and three big, flat stones. Then get us some sticks for a fire.

Narrator: The people ran to get a pot, water, and sticks. Then they got three big, flat stones.

The travelers put the water and stones in the pot. They lit a fire under the pot. The fire cooked the stone soup.

Third Traveler: *(tasting the soup)* M-m-m! The soup is good now. But green beans and a turnip would make it better.

Second Woman: You're right! The wolf didn't eat all of my green beans. I'll run home to get what's left.

Narrator: The woman ran home and took the beans from under the hay.

Third Woman: And I have a turnip.

Narrator: The woman ran home and took the turnip from a basket. The beans and the turnip were put into the pot.

Second Traveler: M-m-m! Smell the soup! It's better now. But peas and beets would make it even better. Can you find some?

First Man: The wolf didn't eat all my peas and beets. I think I still have some at my house. (*Runs off to get them. Comes back.*) Here. (*Puts peas and beets into pot.*)

First Traveler: M-m-m! Smell the soup now. It's much better. But meat would make it much, much better. That will make it the finest soup in the land.

First Woman: I can find some meat. (*Runs off. Comes back with meat. Puts it in the pot.*)

Narrator: Other people went to get food, too. They put it into the pot. Soon the soup was ready to eat.

People of the Village: M-m-m!

Three Travelers: M-m-m! This soup is the best in the land!

Second Man: You are wise men to make soup from stones.

Narrator: But even wise men need sleep. So the people gave their new friends beds for the night. The next morning the travelers woke up and set off down the road again to the next village.

People of the Village: Thank you! Thank you! Goodbye!

Travelers: Goodbye!

IN RESPONSE

Stone soup is a funny kind of soup.

What funny soup could you make?

Make a list of what you would put in your soup.

Give your soup a funny name.

Peanut Butter Soup
peanut Butter
Carrots
Milk
Butter
Ice cream

lemon Soup
lemon
Oranges
Sour candy
limes

Rabbit's Last Race

A Tale from Mexico
told by Pleasant DeSpain

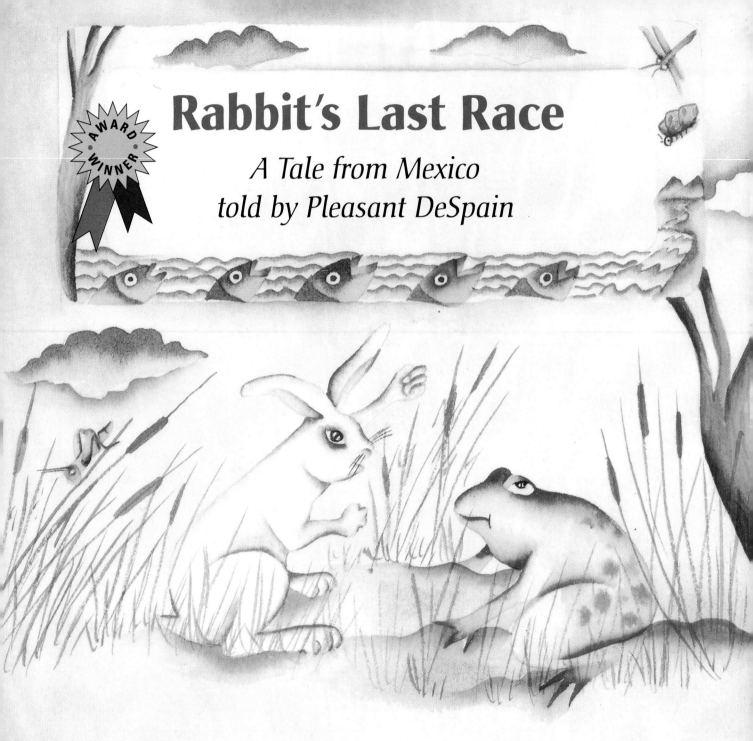

Rabbit loved to brag about how fast he could run. One day Frog got tired of hearing him. So he asked Rabbit to race.

Rabbit wanted to race right away. But Frog
said, "I am a swimmer, not a runner. I need
three days to practice."

Rabbit let Frog choose where they would
race. Frog said, "Let's race from the hill to
the river." The land from hill to river was
covered by tall swamp grass.

Three days passed. Frog did not practice
running. Instead, he made a plan. He called
together all the little frogs in the river. He
talked to almost four hundred frogs! He lined
them up in the tall grass, one good leap
apart, all the way from the hill to the river.
Then he said to Rabbit, "I'm ready."

Frog and Rabbit lined up side by side. Pack Rat brought his tail to the ground with a snap! Off went Rabbit like a shot!

He ran a long way before he looked back. He was sure he was far ahead. But just then he saw Frog jump out of the grass right beside him!

Rabbit thought that just one frog was racing.
He did not know that each frog took one big
leap to the next frog. Rabbit ran like the wind!
"No frog can run as fast as this!" he said.

The river was soon in sight. Rabbit put on
a final burst of speed. But Frog was always
one jump ahead. At the finish line Frog jumped
into the river, shouting "You are too slow, my
friend!"

Rabbit was going too fast to stop.
Ker-splash! He went flying into the river.
When he crawled out, he was tired,
disappointed, and very, very wet.

It was a long time before anyone heard
Rabbit brag about how fast he could run.

Meet the Author and Illustrator

Mwenye Hadithi was born in Kenya. He collects stories told in Africa. Then he writes stories based on the tales he collects. His name means "storyteller."

Adrienne Kennaway painted the pictures for this story. She has worked with Mwenye Hadithi to make other books, too. Adrienne grew up in Kenya and has spent much time painting pictures of this beautiful country.

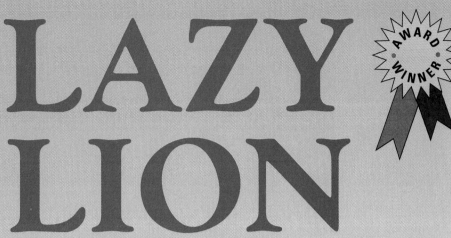

LAZY
LION

by Mwenye Hadithi

illustrated by Adrienne Kennaway

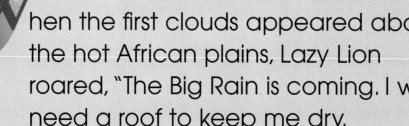

When the first clouds appeared above the hot African plains, Lazy Lion roared, "The Big Rain is coming. I will need a roof to keep me dry.

And since I am the King of the Beasts,
I will order a fine house to be built."

So he went to the White Ants.
        "Build me a house," he ordered.
    "A big house!"

The White Ants built a palace of
towers and turrets and chimneys and
spires.

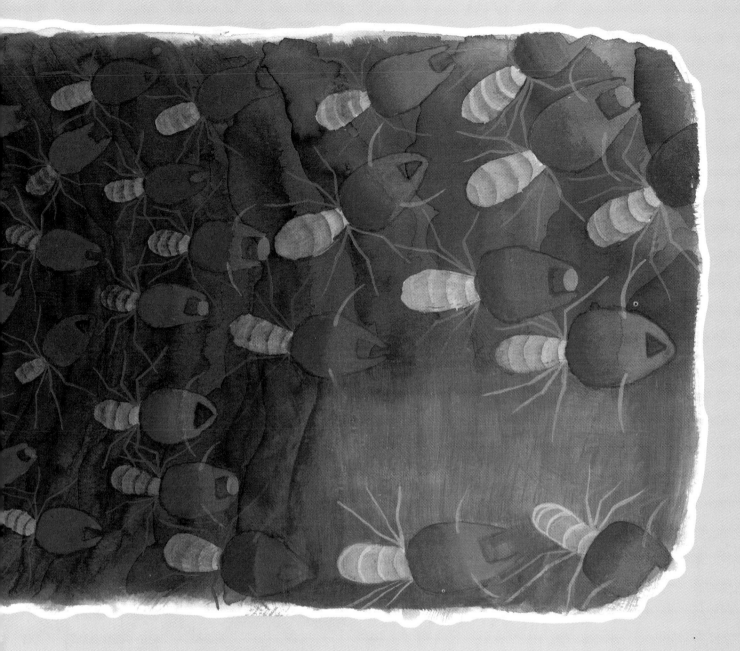

Ｂut Lazy Lion was too big to fit through the door.

"I won't live in the earth," said Lion crossly.

So he went to the Weaver Birds.
"Build me a house," he ordered.
"A big house!"
The Weaver Birds built a nest of
grasses and palm-leaves and soft fluffy

seeds, and it hung from the branch of
a thorn tree. But Lazy Lion was too
heavy to reach the door.

"I won't live up a tree," said Lion
crossly.

So he went to the Aardvarks.
    "Build me a house," he ordered.
"A big house!"
    The Aardvarks dug a huge hole
with many rooms and caverns and

tunnels and caves. But it was damp
and so dark that Lion couldn't see
anything.

"I won't live underground," said
Lion crossly.

So he went to the Honey Badger.
"Build me a house," he ordered.
"A big house!"

Honey Badger found a hollow tree
stump and ate all the bees and
honeycomb inside it, and cleaned it as
clean as clean, and Lion climbed
inside.

ut his head stuck out of the hole in the top, and his tail stuck out of the hole at the bottom.

"I won't live in a tree stump," said Lion crossly.

So he went to Crocodile.
    "Build me a house," he ordered.
"A big house!"
    Crocodile found a cave in the
river-bank and swept it with his tail,

and Lion walked in and went to sleep.
But in the night the cave filled up
with water from the river.

"I won't live in the water," said Lion
crossly.

B y now Lazy Lion was very, very angry, and the sky was absolutely full of big black clouds. So Lion called all the animals together.

"You must ALL build me a house,"

he ordered. "A VERY, VERY BIG . . ."

But just as he said the words "VERY, VERY BIG," there was a flash of lightning in the sky, and a rumbling of thunder, and suddenly the Big Rain poured down everywhere.

The Aardvarks rushed underground.
Honey Badger trundled off to his tree
stump, and Crocodile waddled into his
cave.

The White Ants marched off down their hole. The Weaver Birds flapped to their nest.

And they all watched Lion sitting in the rain in the middle of the African plain.

"He is so very difficult to please," said
Crocodile, snik-snakking his teeth. And
he cried a few tears. Not real ones.
Just little crocodile ones.

And to this day, Lion has not found a house to live in. So he just wanders the African plain. On sunny days and cloudy days. And even in the Big Rains.

What kind of home
would you build for Lion?

Make a home for Lion.
Tell why you think it
would be a good home
for him.

The Lion Roars with a Fearful Sound

The lion roars with a fearful sound,
Roar, roar, roar!

The lion creeps, its prey to catch,
Creep, creep, creep!

The lion pounces with a mighty leap,
Leap, leap, leap!

The lion eats with a crunching sound,
Crunch, crunch, crunch!

The lion sleeps with a gentle snore,
Snore, snore, snore!

by Mabel Segun

Theme Trade Book

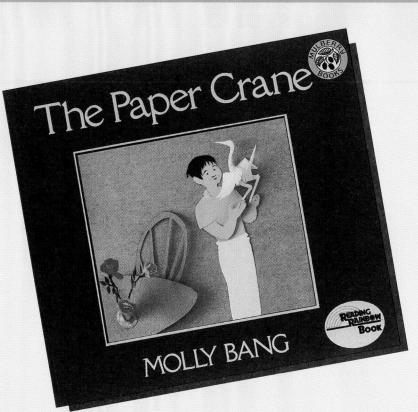

The Paper Crane

by Molly Bang, Greenwillow Books, 1987

A restaurant owner is kind to a hungry man and is paid back in a wonderful way.

More Books for You to Enjoy

The Big Green Bean

by Marcia Wiesbauer, illustrated by Trina Schart Hyman, Silver Press, 1995

An old man and his wife give the queen a giant green bean and get a big surprise in return.

"Charlie Needs a Cloak"

by Tomie dePaola, Simon & Schuster Books for Young Readers, 1973

Charlie makes a new cloak.

Oh, A-Hunting We Will Go

by John Langstaff, illustrated by Nancy Winslow Parker, Aladdin Books, 1974

Based on a favorite old song, this book shows the animals that the children catch.

Watch Me Grow!

Sherry age 5

Nicol age

Tucker 1

Paula age 7

Lisa age 4

Justin age 1

Becky age 5

An

eila

Angela Johnson
asked for a diary when she was nine. She wrote in it every day and has been writing ever since. She likes to write stories about families who care about each other. She is very close to her own family.

David Soman
has illustrated several books by Angela Johnson. His pictures show how the people in the stories care about each other. He also shows us what they are feeling.

The Leaving Morning

story by ANGELA JOHNSON

paintings by DAVID SOMAN

AWARD WINNER

THE LEAVING happened on a soupy, misty morning, when you could hear the street sweeper. Sssshhhshsh....

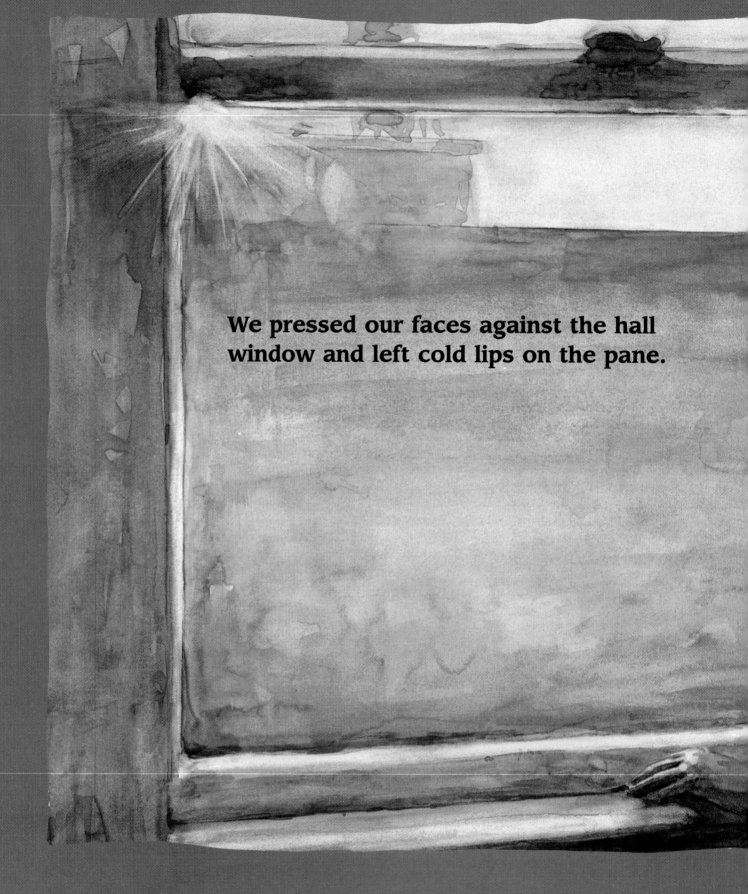

We pressed our faces against the hall
window and left cold lips on the pane.

It was the leaving morning.
Boxes of clothes,
toys,
dishes,
and pictures of us everywhere.

The leaving had been long because we'd packed
days before and said good-bye
to everybody we knew....

Our friends....

The grocer . . . .

Everybody in our building....

And the cousins, especially the cousins.
We said good-bye to the cousins all day long.

Mama said the people in a truck would move us
and take care of everything we loved,
on the leaving morning.

We woke up early and had hot cocoa from the deli across the street.
I made more lips on the deli window
and watched for the movers on the leaving morning.

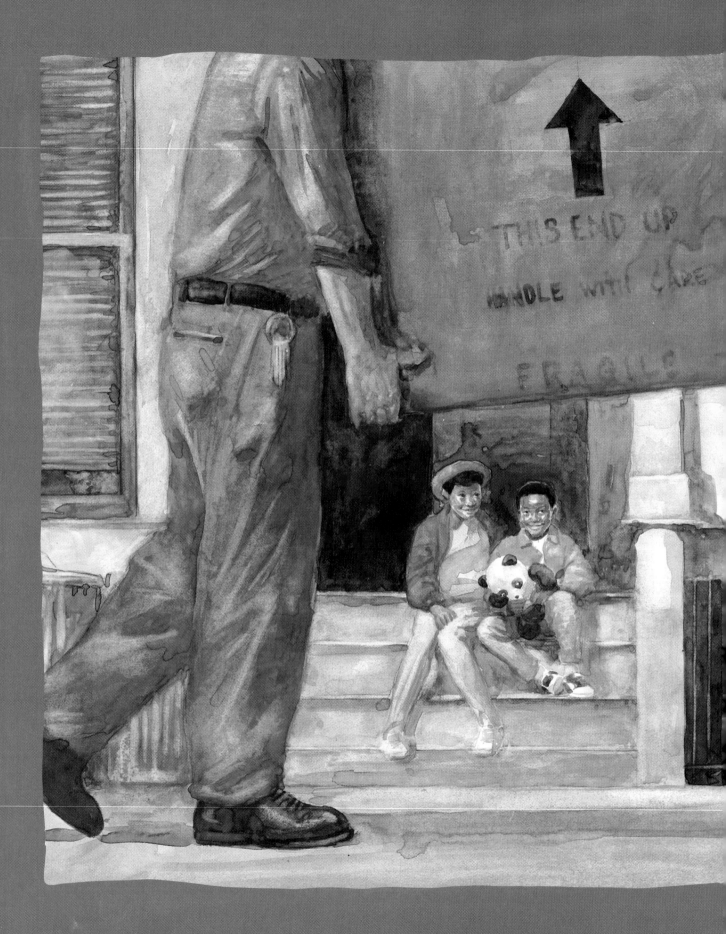

We sat on the steps and
watched the movers.
They had blue moving clothes on and
made bumping noises on the stairs.
There were lots of whistles
and "Watch out, kids."

Got me a moving hat and a kiss on the head
from Miss Mattie, upstairs.
And on the leaving morning she told me
to watch myself in the new place when I crossed
the street, and think of her.

I sat between my mama and daddy, holding their hands.
My daddy said in a little while we'd be someplace we'd love.

So I left lips on the front window
of our apartment,
and said good-bye to our old place,
on the leaving morning.

The children in the story are moving to a new place. How could you make a new student at your school feel welcome?

Discuss your ideas with a friend. Choose one idea and write about it.

Two Ways to Keep in Touch

By Mail

Adam writes to Rosa.

He mails the letter.

Now Adam can take
the letter home.

Adam wants a
copy of the letter.

The mail is sent
by airplane.

The letter arrives
at Rosa's house.

By Computer
Rosa writes back to Adam.

Rosa's letter arrives
at Adam's school.

Meet the Author

Elizabeth Winthrop was the only girl in a family of six children. Her father was a famous newspaper writer.

Ms. Winthrop writes about feelings she had when she was a child. She thinks that children today have the same kinds of feelings. She also thinks children like to read about what they feel.

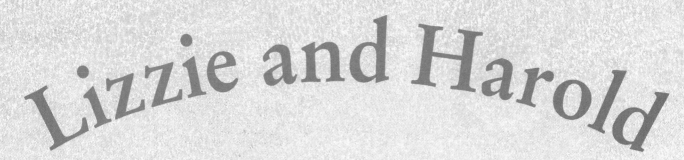

Lizzie and Harold

by Elizabeth Winthrop
illustrated by Martha Weston

More than anything else, Lizzie wanted a best friend.

"How do you get a best friend?" she asked her mother.

"You don't really *get* a best friend," her mother answered. "Usually they just happen if you wait."

But Lizzie did not want to wait.

She wanted a best friend right away.

"Today I am going to find my best friend,"
Lizzie told Harold.

Harold lived next door. Every day they walked
to school together.

"Why do you want a best friend?" Harold asked.

"Because I need someone to tell secrets to and
I want someone to teach me cat's cradle and I want
someone who likes me as much as I like her," Lizzie said.

"I'll be your best friend," Harold said.

"You can't be," Lizzie said. "You're a boy."

"So what?" said Harold.

But Lizzie did not answer.

The next day Lizzie wore a pink flowered dress
and black party shoes to school. Her hair was tied
in two ponytails with pink ribbons.

"You look funny," Harold said.

"I look like Christina," Lizzie answered.
"She is going to be my new best friend."

"I like you best when you look like Lizzie,"
Harold said.

When Lizzie got to school, she ran up to Christina.

"Hello," said Lizzie. "I'm wearing my hair just like yours."

Christina did not answer.

"I'm wearing a dress and party shoes just like you," said Lizzie. "I brought a piece of string so you could teach me cat's cradle. I want you to be my best friend."

"I don't want a best friend," Christina said.

"You don't?" said Lizzie.

"No," said Christina.

She walked away.

"How's your new friend?" Harold asked on the way home.

"Don't ask," said Lizzie. "Christina's not my best friend after all."

"That was quick," said Harold.

"I have a new idea," Lizzie said.

"What is it?" Harold asked.

"You'll see," said Lizzie.

The next day, Lizzie put a sign on the front door
of her house.

The doorbell rang. Lizzie ran to open it.

There stood Harold.

"Here I am," he said.
"Your new best friend."

"You can't be my best friend," Lizzie said.
"You're a boy, and you're only five and three quarters."

"I learned how to do cat's cradle," Harold said.

"You did?" Lizzie said. "Can you teach it to me?"

"Sure," Harold said.

"I'll teach you Jacob's Ladder and Teacup and Saucer and Witch's Hat tomorrow," Harold said.

Nobody else rang the doorbell.

Lizzie took down the sign.

"Does that mean I'm your best friend now?"
Harold asked.

"No," said Lizzie. "That means I give up.
I don't want a best friend after all."

The next day Harold was carrying a big blue bag
to school.

"What's in your bag?" asked Lizzie.

"It's my trick-or-treat candy," said Harold.

"Why are you taking it to school?" asked Lizzie.

"I'm going to give it to the person who promises to be
my best friend," said Harold. "Since you don't want to
be my best friend, I'm going to find somebody else."

"Harold, you can't find a best friend that way,"
Lizzie said.

"Why not?" asked Harold.

"Because best friends just happen to you. You can't go
out and buy them. Besides, I thought you wanted to be
my best friend," Lizzie cried.

But Harold wasn't listening.

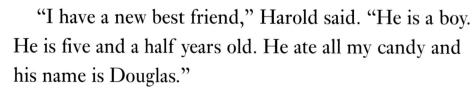

All day long Lizzie thought about Harold. When she met him after school, he did not have his blue bag of candy.

"I have a new best friend," Harold said. "He is a boy. He is five and a half years old. He ate all my candy and his name is Douglas."

"Why do you look so sad?" Lizzie asked.
"Because I like you better," said Harold.

"Well, I have a new best friend too," Lizzie said.

"He is a boy. He is five and three quarters years old. He knows how to do cat's cradle and he likes me as much as I like him."

Harold looked even sadder.

"What's his name?" Harold asked.

"Harold," said Lizzie.

Why do you think Lizzie and Harold are friends?

What can you do to show someone you are a friend?

Talk about your ideas.

Make a list with a partner about how to be a friend.

How to Be a Friend

1. Share with others
2. You
3. _____
4. _____
5. _____
6. _____

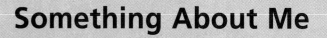

Something About Me

There's something about me
That I'm knowing.
There's something about me
That isn't showing.

I'm growing!

Anonymous

Good-bye, Six—Hello, Seven

I'm getting a higher bunk bed.
And I'm getting a bigger bike.
And I'm getting to cross Connecticut Avenue
   all by myself, if I like.
And I'm getting to help do dishes.
And I'm getting to weed the yard.
And I'm getting to think that seven
   could be hard.

by Judith Viorst

Meet Marc Brown

Marc Brown's grandmother told him wonderful stories when he was a child. He began to tell stories to his son, too. One night, he made up a story about an aardvark who didn't like his nose. That became the first *Arthur* book. Now there are more than twenty books about Arthur.

"You've been looking at puppies for months,"
said D.W.
"When are you going to ask Mom and Dad
if you can have one?"
"I'm waiting for just the right moment,"
said Arthur, "so promise not to say anything!"

That night at dinner, Father asked,
"What's new?"
"Arthur wants a puppy," said D.W.
"Blabbermouth!" said Arthur.

"A puppy is a big responsibility," said Father.
"I can take care of it," said Arthur.
"We'll think about it," Mother said.
"That means no," explained D.W.

After dinner Mother and Father did the dishes.
"Can you hear what they're saying?" asked Arthur.
"They're worried about the new carpet," whispered D.W.
Suddenly the door opened.

"We've decided you may have a puppy if you can take care of it," said Father.

"Wow!" said Arthur.

"*But*," said Mother, "first you need to show us you're responsible."

"How will I ever prove I'm responsible?" asked Arthur.
"The best way I know is to get a job," said D.W.
"Then you can pay back the seven dollars you owe me!"
"Ka-chingg!" went her cash register.

Arthur wondered what kind of
job he could do.
"You could work for my dad
at the bank," said Muffy.
"He needs some new tellers."

"If I were you, I'd get a job
at Joe's Junk Yard crushing
old cars," offered Binky Barnes.

"Do something that *you* like,"
said Francine.
That gave Arthur an idea.

179

"I'll take care of other people's pets," said Arthur, "then Mom and Dad will know I can take care of my own."

Arthur and Francine put up signs to advertise his new business.

His family helped, too.

Arthur waited and waited. Then, just before bedtime, the phone rang.

"Hello," he said. "Arthur's Pet Business. How may I help you?

"Yes. No. When? Where? Great!" said Arthur.

"Hooray! I'm going to watch Mrs. Wood's dog while she's on vacation, and I'll earn ten dollars!"
"Oh, no!" said D.W. "Not nasty little Perky?"
"Isn't that the dog the mailman calls 'JAWS'?" asked Father.
"That's Perky!" said D.W.

The next morning, Arthur ran all the way to
Mrs. Wood's house.
"Right on time!" said Mrs. Wood.
"*Grrrrr*," growled Perky.

"She hasn't been herself lately," said Mrs. Wood.
"I'm worried."

"I'll take good care of her," said Arthur.
"We'll be best friends."

"*Grrrrr*," growled Perky.

"Here's her schedule and a list of things
she doesn't like," said Mrs. Wood.
"I'll see you next Sunday."

Arthur did his best to make
Perky feel at home.
Every day he brushed her.
He tried to fix her
favorite foods.
They took lots of long walks—
day and night.
Perky made sure they had the whole
sidewalk to themselves.

"You look exhausted," said Mother. "Maybe taking
care of a dog is too much work . . ."
"Any dog I get will be easier than Perky,"
said Arthur.

PERKY'S
TOY BOX

Word of Arthur's pet business got around.
On Monday the MacMillans asked Arthur to watch
their canary, Sunny.

On Tuesday Prunella gave Arthur
her ant farm.

On Wednesday the Brain asked
Arthur to take care of his frogs
while he went on vacation.

Best of all, on Thursday The Amazing Larry
asked Arthur to keep Cuddles,
his trained boa constrictor.

Animals were everywhere
—until Mother put her foot down.
"I want all these animals in the basement *now!*"
she ordered.

By bedtime all the pets were downstairs.
All except Perky.
Perky slept in Arthur's room.

On Saturday Buster asked Arthur to go to the movies. "I can't," said Arthur. "When I finish cleaning these cages, it will be feeding time.

"And anyway, it's Perky's last night with me and she seems sick. I don't want to leave her."

"Well, I bet you're happy today," said D.W.
the next morning.
"You get rid of Perky and collect ten dollars!"
"I can't believe it," said Arthur.
"But I'm going to miss Perky."

"Arthur, Mrs. Wood just called to say she's on her way over," said Mother.
"Now, wait here, Perky," ordered Arthur.
"I'll go and get your leash."

When Arthur went back into the kitchen,
Perky was gone.
"Here Perky! Perky!" called Arthur.
But Perky didn't come.
"She's not in the basement," called Father.
"She's not in the backyard," said D.W.
"She's lost!" said Arthur.
"Oh, oh!" said D.W. "You're in big trouble!"

"Arthur, Mrs. Wood is here!" called Mother.

"Hi, Mrs. Wood," said D.W. "Guess what? Arthur lost Perky!"

"My poor darling is lost?" asked Mrs. Wood.

"Don't worry," said Father. "Arthur's looking for her right now."

Suddenly they heard a bark.

"Everybody come quick!" called Arthur.

"Look," said Arthur. "Perky's had puppies!"
"No wonder she's been acting so strange,"
said Mrs. Wood.
"You've done a wonderful job taking care of Perky,
when she needed a friend the most.
How can I ever thank you?"

"A reward might be nice," suggested D.W.

"Shush!" said Mother.

"Here's the money I owe you," said Mrs. Wood.

"And, how would you like to keep one of Perky's puppies as a special thank you?"

"I'd love to," said Arthur. "If I'm allowed."

"Of course," said Mother. "You've earned it."

"Wow!" said Arthur.
"Ten dollars *and* my very own puppy!
I can't believe it!"
"Neither can I," said D.W. "Now you can finally pay back my seven dollars."
"Ka-chingg!" went her cash register.

IN RESPONSE

Arthur showed he was responsible when he took care of all the pets. How did he take care of them?

Do you take care of something at home or at school?

Draw a picture of something you take care of.
Write about how you do it.

Watch Us Grow

All animals change as they grow. They get bigger and stronger every day.

A newborn puppy cannot see or hear.

Puppies are very playful.

It takes about a year for a puppy to grow as big as its mother.

204

A newborn kitten cannot
see, hear, or walk.

As kittens grow,
they become very
playful.

By the time a cat is
one year old, it is
grown-up.

Pets Need Care

Different kinds of pets need different things.
Some pets need a lot of care, and some need very little.
It is important to be gentle with all pets.

Dogs are great pets, but they need lots of care and training.
Dogs are fun pets because they like to please people.

Taking Care of Fluffy
Monday
Tuesday
Wednesday
Thursday
Friday
Weekend
Carlos
Beth
John
Kim
Fred
Julia
Play
Jenny
Lisa
Seth
Nan
Max
Dan
Inez
Ben
Dana
Rob

This guinea pig is a classroom pet. The children in the class take turns feeding him and taking him home on weekends.

Lizards are easy to take care of. They like to eat insects and plants. Like all pets, they need fresh water every day.

Theme Trade Book

Pablo's Tree

by Pat Mora, illustrated by Cecily Lang, Macmillan, 1994

Each year Pablo's grandfather helps him celebrate his birthday in a special way.

More Books for You to Enjoy

The Big Seed

by Ellen Howard, illustrated by Lillian Hoban, Simon & Schuster, 1993

The seeds that Beth plants surprise everyone—even her!

Duncan & Dolores

by Barbara Samuels, Macmillan, 1986

In this funny story, Dolores learns how to take care of her new cat.

Wilson Sat Alone

by Debra Hess, illustrated by Diane Greenseid, Simon & Schuster Books for Young Readers, 1994

Wilson always sat alone at school. Things change when a new girl joins the class.

aardvarks

Aardvarks are African animals with big ears and long heads with piglike noses. **Aardvarks** use their long tongues for catching ants.

aardvark

apartment

An **apartment** is a room or many rooms to live in. Our **apartmen**t has a living room, kitchen, three bedrooms, and one bathroom.

apartment

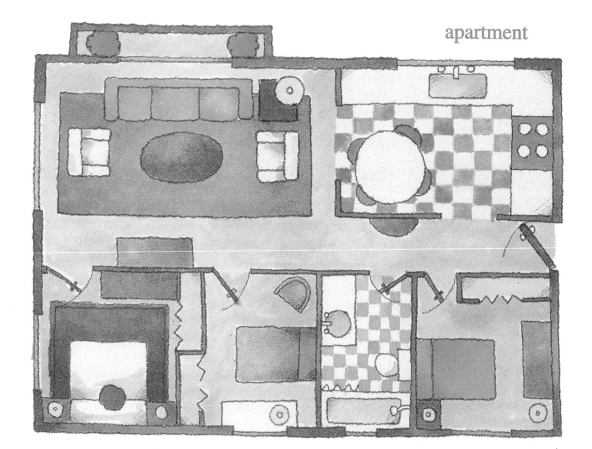

awake

Awake means to come out of sleep, to wake up. The baby is wide **awake** after her nap.

awake

Bb

beets

Beets are vegetables with round, red roots that are eaten. Her favorite vegetables are **beets** and peas.

beets

business

A **business** is a person's work or job. She has lots of customers in her baby-sitting **business**.

Cc

canary

A **canary** is a small, yellow songbird that is often kept as a pet. The **canary** sings for me in the morning.

canary

careful

Careful means taking care not to make mistakes. The children were **careful** not to get their new clothes dirty.

cave

caves

Caves are openings in hillsides or under the ground. Bats live inside dark and damp **caves**.

council

A **council** is a group of people who meet to plan or decide things. The city **council** met to plan a special event.

council

cousins

Cousins are sons or daughters of one's uncle or aunt. My aunt and my **cousins** visit us every summer.

crocodile

crocodile

A **crocodile** is a large, cold-blooded animal with thick, scaly skin, a long body, a pointed snout, and four short legs. The **crocodile** stays close to the river.

dollars

Dollars are money made of paper or coins and are worth one hundred cents each. I saved five **dollars** in my piggy bank.

dollars

earn

Earn means to receive pay for work done. Ann is working hard to **earn** some money.

elder

elders

Elders are older people. Kendra learned a lot from listening to stories the **elders** told.

explained

Explained means told the reason for or made clear. The coach **explained** why he was late for the game.

favorite

Favorite means the thing one likes best of all. Red is my **favorite** color.

finish line

The **finish line** is the place marked to show where a race ends. José was the first to cross the **finish line**.

finish line

Foolish means silly. Jamie acted very **foolish** in front of his friends.

grocer

A **grocer** is a person who sells food. The **grocer** in my neighborhood sells fresh fruit.

grocer

hair

hair

Hair is a mass of threadlike growths that covers a person's or animal's skin. Both girls had long black **hair**.

---

job

A **job** is work done for pay. Mandy was paid two dollars a week for her **job** as a dog sitter.

junk yard

A **junk yard** is a place where old metal, paper, and old cars are sorted and stored. Chet's father took pipes to the **junk yard**.

lazy

Ll

lazy

Lazy means not willing to work hard. The cat felt **lazy** in the heat of the sun.

Mm

meadows

Meadows are fields of grass. The children played in the **meadows** behind the barn.

meadows

moment

A **moment** is a very short time. Ima will be back in just a **moment**.

palm-leaves

palm-leaves

Palm-leaves are the large leaves of trees that grow in warm places. **Palm-leaves** moved with the wind.

puppies

puppies

Puppies are young dogs. The dog keeps her **puppies** close to her.

quick

Quick means fast or with speed. Get your coat and come **quick!**

rattlesnake

A **rattlesnake** is a poisonous snake that has hard rings that make a rattling noise at the end of its tail. We saw and heard a **rattlesnake** nearby.

rattlesnake

responsibility

Responsibility is something or someone to be taken care of. It is Jack's **responsibility** to take care of his puppy.

reward

A **reward** is money that is given in return for some kind of help or good work. The woman gave the boy a **reward** for finding her lost kitten.

Ss

scare

Scare means to frighten or become afraid. That mask will **scare** everyone.

scare

secrets

Secrets are something told to someone special and hidden from others. You can tell your **secrets** to a good friend.

spires

Spires are parts of buildings that come to a point at the top. The **spires** on the building reached up into the sky.

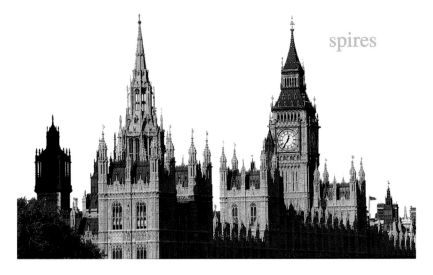

spires

street sweeper

A **street sweeper** is a machine that sweeps the dirt off the street. The **street sweeper** came down our street early in the morning.

street sweeper

swamp grass

Swamp grass is grass that grows in and around wet, marshy land. The frogs hid in the tall **swamp grass**.

swimmer

swimmer

A **swimmer** is someone who swims in the water. Danny was a good **swimmer**.

Tt

tunnels

Tunnels are underground or underwater openings that some animals make. Aardvarks make **tunnels** for their homes.

tunnel

turnip

A **turnip** is a plant with a round, white or yellow root that is eaten as a vegetable. We had turkey and **turnips** for supper.

turnips

turrets

Turrets are small towers on a building. The castle had many **turrets**.

turrets

- -

Uu

usually
Usually means most often. The bus **usually** gets to school on time.

vacation

A **vacation** is a time when one stops working or going to school to rest and play. When school is out, I'm going on **vacation**.

warn

Warn means to tell about a danger before it happens. The new sign will **warn** people not to feed the bears in the park.

warn

weaver bird

weaver birds

Weaver birds are kinds of birds that make fancy woven nests and live mostly in Africa. Male **weaver birds** build the nests.

wolf

A **wolf** is a wild animal that looks like a dog. The **wolf** ran after the little rabbit.

wolf

wonderful

Wonderful means very good or excellent. The pie was so **wonderful** that they ate it all up.

- -

Yy

young

Someone is **young** when they are in the early years of life. The **young** boy is playing with his new blocks.

young

223

ACKNOWLEDGMENTS

Grateful acknowledgment is made to the following publishers, authors, and agents for their permission to reprint copyrighted material. Every effort has been made to locate all copyright proprietors; any errors or omissions in copyright notice are inadvertent and will be corrected in future printings as they are discovered.

Arthur's Pet Business: An Arthur Adventure by Marc Brown. Copyright ©1990 by Marc Brown. Reprinted by permission of Little, Brown and Company, and of the author's agent, Rosenstone/Wender.

Baby Rattlesnake told by Te Ata. Adapted by Lynn Moroney. Illustrated by Veg Reisberg. Story copyright ©1989 by Lynn Moroney. Illustrations copyright ©1989 by Veg Reisberg. Reprinted by permission of Children's Book Press.

"Good-Bye, Six–Hello, Seven" from **If I Were In Charge of the World and Other Worries** by Judith Viorst. Illustrated by Lynne Cherry. Copyright ©1981 by Judith Viorst. Reprinted by permission of the American publisher, Atheneum Books for Young Readers, an imprint of Simon & Schuster Children's Publishing Division, of the British publisher, Lescher & Lescher, Ltd., and of the Australian publisher, Ashton Scholastic.

Lazy Lion by Mwenye Hadithi. Illustrated by Adrienne Kennaway. Copyright ©1990 by Bruce Hobson and Adrienne Kennaway. Reprinted by permission of the American publisher, Little, Brown and Company, and of the British publisher, Hodder & Stoughton Limited.

The Leaving Morning story by Angela Johnson. Paintings by David Soman. Text copyright ©1992 by Angela Johnson. Illustrations copyright ©1992 by David Soman. Reprinted by permission of Orchard Books, New York.

"The Lion Roars with a Fearful Sound" by Mabel Segun. Copyright © Mabel Segun. Reprinted by permission of the author.

Lizzie and Harold by Elizabeth Winthrop. Illustrated by Martha Weston. Text copyright ©1986 by Elizabeth Winthrop Mahony. Illustrations copyright ©1986 by Martha Weston. Reprinted by permission of Lothrop, Lee & Shepard Books, a division of William Morrow & Company, Inc.

Phonetic respelling system from **The World Book Encyclopedia.** ©1995 World Book, Inc. By permission of the publisher.

COVER: Cover photography ©1996 by Jade Albert Studio. Cover illustration ©1996 by Kathi Ember. Cover design, art direction and production by Design Five.

ILLUSTRATION: 8–9, Tyrone Geter; 46–60, Esther Baran; 62–67, Leovigildo Martinez Torres; 99, David Danz; 110–111, Ellen Sasaki; 168–169, Sally Vitsky; 204–205, Kathy Hendrikson.

GLOSSARY ILLUSTRATION: 210, Nan Brooks; 211, Daniel Powers; 212, Juliette Borda (Top), James Edwards (Bottom); 214, Lee Steadman (Top), Christa Kieffer (Bottom); 216, Kim Howard (Top), Carol Inouye (Bottom); 217, Michele Noiset; 219, David Gothard; 220, Rae Ecklund (Top), Roz Schanzer (Bottom); 221, Eileen Hine; 223, Lee Steadman.

PHOTOGRAPHY: Unless otherwise indicated, photographs of book covers and of children's art were provided by Ulsaker Studio, Inc. Background photograph for Silver Bookcase by Allan Penn for SBG. Credits listed below for children's art indicate the name of the artist. The abbreviation SBG stands for Silver Burdett Ginn. 4–5, (background) Allan Penn for SBG, 10, (t.) courtesy Children's Book Press, (m.) courtesy Lynn Moroney; 12–39, (background) Allan Penn for SBG; 41, courtesy Hiawatha Estes; 42, University of Science and Arts of Oklahoma; 43, courtesy Hiawatha Estes; 44, pottery storyteller figures by Helen Cordero, Cochiti Pueblo, New Mexico, courtesy The Heard Museum, Phoenix, Arizona, photo by Jerry Jacka; 45, (t. l.) pottery storyteller figure by Rose Pecos, Jemez Pueblo, courtesy The Heard Museum Gift Shop, Phoenix, Arizona, photo by Jerry Jacka, (b. r.) pottery storyteller figure by Helen Cordero, from the Girard Foundation Collection in the Museum of International Folk Art, a unit of the Museum of New Mexico, Santa Fe, New Mexico, photo by Michel Monteaux; 46, (t.) © Mitchell Sharmat, (m.) courtesy Mitchell Sharmat, (b.) courtesy Esther Baran; 61, Dave Bradley for SBG; 98, Jeffrey Dunn for SBG; 102–103, Doug Mindell for SBG; 104, (l., r.) courtesy Orchard Books; 104–105, Allan Penn for SBG; 133, George Disario for SBG; 134, Allan Penn for SBG; 135, Doug Mindell for SBG; 136, courtesy Holiday House; 170, courtesy Little, Brown, and Co., Inc., 170–171, Allan Penn for SBG; 203, Doug Mindell for SBG; 206, © David Delossy/The Image Bank; 207, (t.) George Disario for SBG; (b.) Dave Bradley for SBG; 210, © N. Myers/Bruce Coleman, Inc.; 211, (m.) Allan Penn for SBG, (b.) © Jane Burton/Bruce Coleman, Inc.; 213, (t.) © David M. Dennis/Tom Stack & Associates, (m.) Allan Penn for SBG; 215, (t.) © 1987 Blair Seitz/Photo Researchers, Inc., (b.) Dave Bradley for SBG; 217, © S. Achernar/The Image Bank; 218, (t.) © G. C. Kelley/Photo Researchers, Inc., (b.) Doug Mindell for SBG; 219, © Porterfield/Chickering/Photo Researchers, Inc.; 221, Allan Penn for SBG; 222, © M. Reardon/Photo Researchers, Inc.; 223, © Victoria Hurst, Tom Stack & Associates for SBG